In the FIDDLE Is a SONG

A LIFT-THE-FLAP BOOK OF HIDDEN POTENTIAL

BY DURGA BERNHARD

chronicle books · san francisco

In the acorn

In the larva

is a plum
waiting for
the sun.

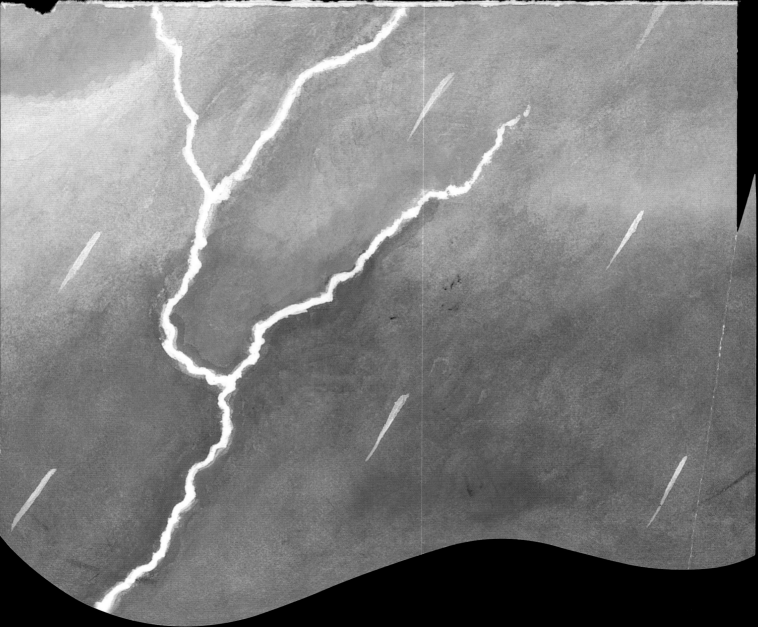

is a storm

waiting to
bring rain.

In the blossom

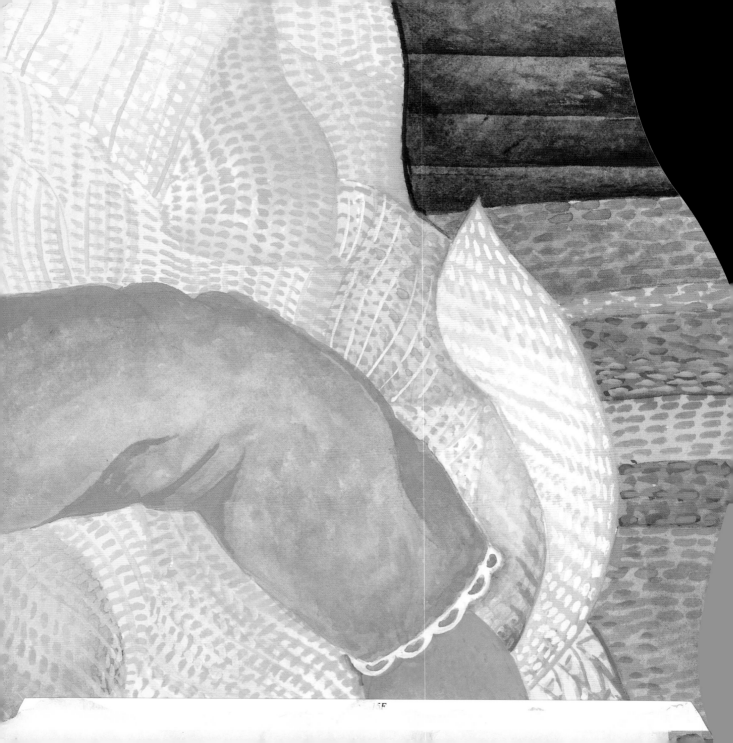

is a **weaving**

waiting to
be spun.

In the cloud

is a **song**

waiting to be played.

In the thread

is **bread**

waiting to
be baked.

In the fiddle

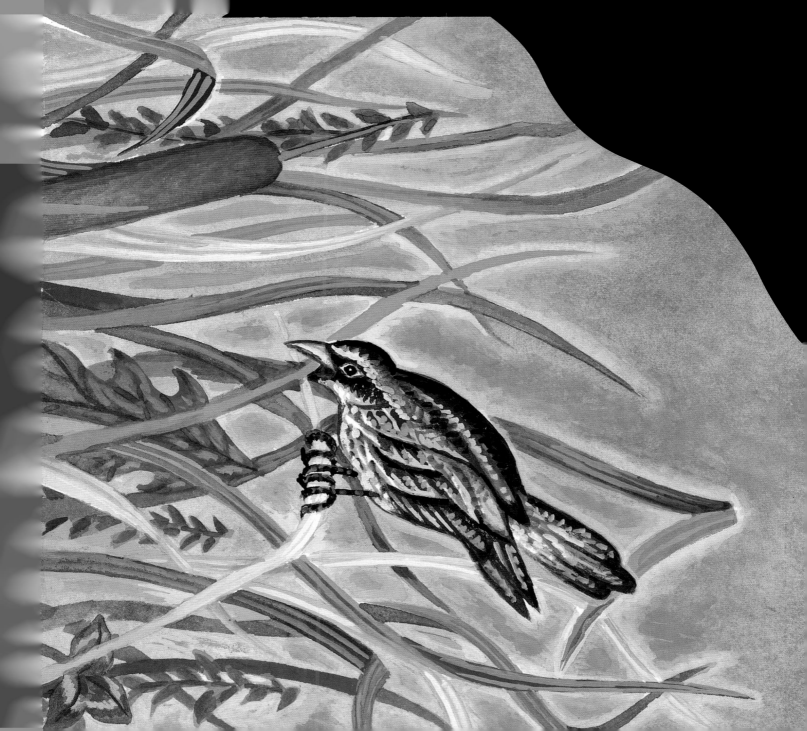

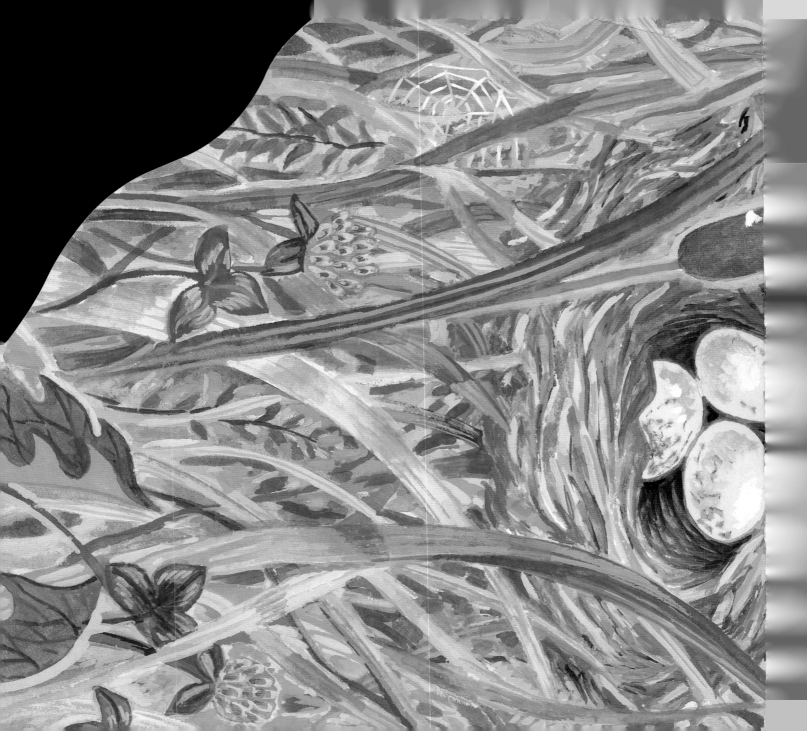

is a **nest**

waiting to
be built.

In the wheat

In the grass

is a pot

waiting to
be shaped.

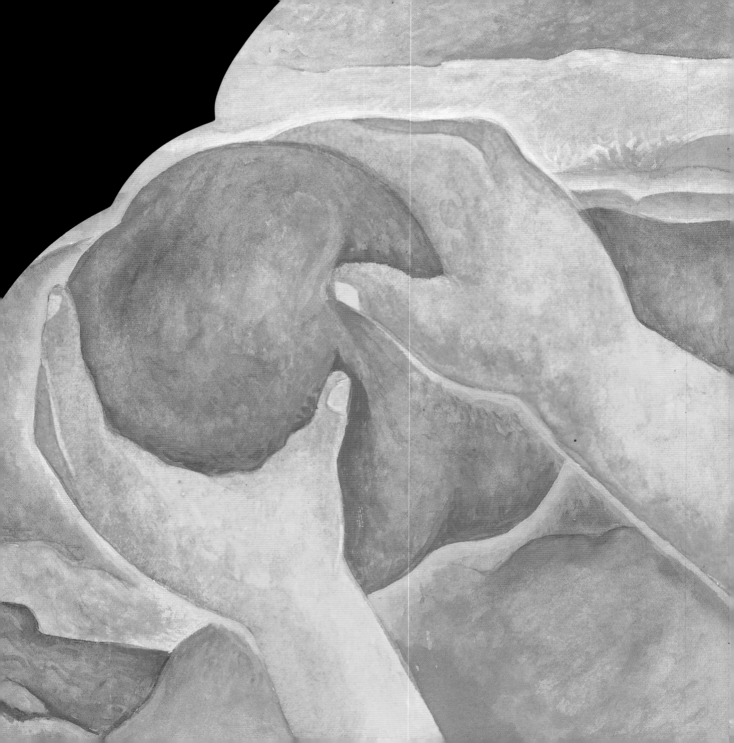

In the clay

is a **tree**
waiting to
grow tall.